The Fear of Being Seen as White Losers
White working-class masculinities
and the killing of Stephen Lawrence

Five Leaves Bookshop Occasional Papers

The Current Status of Jerusalem by Edward Said
978-1-910170-09-0, 32 pages, £4

Doctor Who and the Communist: Malcolm Hulke and his career in television by Michael Herbert
978-1-910170-08-3, 32 pages, £4

Strengthening Democracy in Post-conflict Northern Ireland by Maria Power
978-1-910170-16-8, 32 pages, £4

Anarchy 38: Nottingham by Freedom Press
978-1-910170-18-2, 32 pages, £4

How We Live and How We Might Live by William Morris
978-1-910170-26-7, 28 pages, £4

Harper Lee and the American South by Katie Hamilton
978-1-910170-27-4, 28 pages, £4

That Precious Strand of Jewishness that Challenges Authority by Leon Rosselson
978-1-910170-33-5, 28 pages, £4

Mad John's Walk by John Gallas
978-1-910170-41-0, 16 pages, £3

Street Haunting by Virginia Woolf & **Bulwell** by Stanley Middleton
978-1-910170-42-7, 24 pages, £4

The Mask of Anarchy by Percy Bysshe Shelley
978-1-910170-48-9, 24 pages, £4

Available from Five Leaves or from other bookshops worldwide.
All prices include UK postage if ordered direct from
Five Leaves Bookshop.

www.fiveleavesbookshop.co.uk

The Fear of Being Seen as White Losers
White working-class masculinities and the killing of Stephen Lawrence

David Jackson

Five Leaves Bookshop Occasional Papers

The Fear of Being Seen as White Losers:
White Working Class Masculinities and the
Killing of Stephen Lawrence
by David Jackson

This essay is a longer version of an essay which first
appeared in *Sosiologi I Dag*, Argang 32,nr.4, 2002

This edition published in 2018
by Five Leaves Bookshop
14a Long Row, Nottingham NG1 2DH
www.fiveleavesbookshop.co.uk
Five Leaves Bookshop Occasional Paper 11
ISBN: 978-1-910170-54-0

Copyright © David Jackson, 2018

Also available by David Jackson from Five Leaves
*Destroying the Baby in Themselves:
Why the two boys killed James Bulger*

Designed and typeset by Five Leaves Bookshop

Printed in Great Britain

The Fear of Being Seen as White Losers: White Working Class Masculinities and the Killing of Stephen Lawrence

Stephen Lawrence was murdered on April 22 1993 as he waited for a bus in Eltham, south-east London, with his friend Duwayne Brooks. The group of young white men shouted, "What, what, nigger?" as they killed the young black man.

A combination of police inadequacy ("... professional incompetence, institutional racism and a failure of leadership by senior officers..." (Macpherson, 1999, p312.)), the failure to bring anyone to justice for the crime, and the emotional bravery and persistence of Stephen's parents, Doreen and Neville Lawrence, finally resulted in a public inquiry chaired by Sir William Macpherson. That Inquiry led to an important period when the issue of racism in public institutions and the underlying reasons for police incompetence in the Stephen Lawrence case were "placed high on the political and media agenda." (see Blair, Gillborn, Kemp and Macdonald (1999).)

I would like to try and extend some of these anti-racist debates by taking a close look at some of the possible reasons why the suspects might have done what they did. But before we look at that, it's important to contextualise the killing of Stephen Lawrence. His murder was a part of the rise of extremely violent racism in Britain (particularly in south-east London) and in Europe over the preceding decade. We need to explore the neglected links between Stephen Lawrence's murder and the wider issues of English national and young white working-class masculine identities to more clearly understand the complex reasons for the killing.

Note that the five suspects have not been proved to have been Stephen Lawrence's murderers, and I do not want to give the impression that it was undoubtedly all five of them who carried out the stabbing. However the police surveillance video transcript has given us detailed evidence of the "sub-culture of obsessive violence, fuelled by racist prejudice and hatred" (Macpherson, 1999, p5) that permeated the everyday lives of the suspects. I agree with the Macpherson report when it says: "If these suspects were not involved there must have been five or six almost identical young thugs at large on the night of 22 April 1993 to commit this terrible racist crime." (Macpherson, 1999, p5.)

Using the police surveillance video transcript and the Martin Bashir interview with the suspects on *Tonight*, we can see how the suspects make sense of their inner and outer worlds. In terms of jobs, income, reputation and style, the suspects' lives are often characterised by uncertainty and anxiety, covered up by brave performances. They have concealed fears of being seen as white 'losers', and fantasised perceptions of being 'ruined' or usurped by a young masculine black presence.

The suspects countered their insecurities about being viewed as failed men through attempting to re-constitute themselves as vigorous, hard and aggressively dominant, especially in their gendered selves and white English identities. So it's possible to argue that the killing of Stephen Lawrence was a defensive bid to counter the imaginary threat of a black menace.

Interrogating White, Racialised, Embodied Masculinities

One way to make sense of the killing of Stephen Lawrence is through a careful analysis of racialised embodied masculinities. As a part of that analysis it's necessary to interrogate some of the gaps, silences and invisibilities that surround white ethnicities and heterosexual embodied masculinities in our contemporary culture. We need to establish explicit links between national identities, race, sexualities and masculine embodiment.

White Ethnicities

One of the main barriers to understanding why the suspects might have done what they did is the invisibility of whiteness, and English whiteness in particular. Whiteness is so taken for granted in our culture that it doesn't seem to exist at all, or, as Richard Dyer suggests, whiteness is "everything and nothing; at the same time." (Dyer, 1997) But there are positive signs that whiteness is being brought into focus as a social and historical phenomenon (Nayak, 1999), so to probe more deeply into the reasons for the murder we need to disturb the established norms of white male culture in England. A crucial part of this critical exposure of whiteness is to show that whiteness is a racialised identity with specific bodily relations. Whiteness is not an essentialised, homogeneous identity, but one which is constructed through relational, dynamic, power-driven social processes. The central racialised masculinities in England — whiteness, Asianness and blackness (Frosh, Phoenix and Pattman, 2002) — are socially produced through the power relations, differences, conflicts and hierarchical divisions between themselves in a wider social and political context. Traditionally and historically in England, taken-for-granted assumptions of white masculine superiority were sustained through the illusion of a cultural homogeneity, that white masculine norms were the only, 'proper' standards of civilised humanity to aspire towards. These supremacist assumptions are now being sharply challenged and changed.

Today there is conflict, ambivalence and insecurity at the heart of white heterosexual English masculinities, which is experienced in bodily and sexualised terms. White men's bodies are threatened by loss, failure and national decline, but also by the disturbing difference and otherness of black bodies. Conversely, whiteness, as a psycho-social shaped identity, depends on non-whites for its sense of self. The social meanings of white English masculinities pivot on the existence of subordinated black masculinities.

From a broader anti-imperialist perspective, the legacies of colonialism are clearly visible within the internal hierarchies between white and black men. Triumphant white English masculine identities are constructed in opposition to racialised, sexualised and subordinated Others (in England, mainly black and Asian). This results in the racist myth of white men as superior, disembodied, civilised and rational; while black men are construed as savage, irrational and sensual. (Messerschmidt, 1998, p134)

From an imperialist vantage point, white men viewed black men as only bodies, not minds. (Rutherford, 1997, p52) Black men's bodies were primarily seen as bestial, unclean, menacing and criminal. (Segal, 1990, p175) The unconscious longings and repressed fantasies of white men were also projected onto black men's sexualities. As a result, many black men were viewed as hyper-sexual beings, representing 'the ultimate in phallic embodiment' (Nayak, 1997) for white, heterosexual men. And that hyper-sexual presence of black men, a product of white men's imaginings, is also what white men, especially in emasculating conditions, secretly desire for themselves.

The white man's invention of black masculinities as an inflated bodily ideal has developed into new forms. Research in 2002 traced some of the ambivalent ways in which white English (London) boys perceive blackness. There was still the threat of masculine inadequacy, of not measuring up to the fantasised projections of black bodily forms, but that has become tinged with a mixture of admiration, envy and antagonism. (Frosh, Phoenix and Pattman, 2002) Les Back has remarked on this combination of fear and fascination that characterises many young, white, English men's perceptions of blackness. (Back, 1994) In *Young Masculinities*, Frosh, Phoenix and Pattman produce more intriguing evidence of this strange, contradictory cocktail of envy, fear and antagonism in white boys and young men. (Frosh, Phoenix and Pattman, 2002) Afro-Caribbean young men are viewed as super-masculine and super-sexual by white English boys, and they seem to take literally young black English men's displays of hardness, coolness, style and sexual prowess. This aggrandised view of young black masculinities deepens the fear and anxieties that many white boys experience about the stability and coherence of their own embodied whiteness.

Embodied, Heterosexual, Working-class Masculinities

It's not only white ethnicities that are perceived to be under threat. The illusory stability of the normative, heterosexual, masculine subject is also being interrogated. A central part of the concealed, taken-for-granted position of the normative masculine subject is a result of the tendency to treat "man as generic human." (Brod, 1987, p40) The over-generalisation, disembodying, de-sexing and rational distancing of white heterosexual men as universal paradigms for human experience has had damaging results for others, and for many such men themselves. Not only have men hogged the central spotlight for too long, in an often aggressive, authoritarian and arrogant manner, but the specific complexity, richness and contradictoriness of men's lived experiences as gendered, social beings has been lost. Once the false screen of "man as generic human" falls away, the detailed and explicit enquiry into the sexed and gendered specificity (Collier, 1997) of embodied, heterosexual masculinities can begin. And this line of enquiry can also start to open up some answers to the dilemmas posed by the killing of Stephen Lawrence.

From this new perspective, the construction of embodied heterosexual masculinities can be understood as the outcome of psycho-social processes that are primarily relational, dynamically interactive, multiple and performative. Masculinities are constructed as relations of power, constituting their own sense of superiority, embodied solidity and boundaried intactness (Theweleit, 1987) through repetitively projecting what they perceive as weak, soft and anxiety-making in themselves onto the subordinated Otherness of blackness, femininity and gayness.

A major part of our critical interrogation of normative masculinities is to contest the disembodied and de-sexed character of taken-for-granted masculine heterosexual identities.

Masculinities aren't natural results of possessing a male body. Literature on the sociology of the body (Morgan, 1993; Connell, 2000; Petersen, 1998) has developed a more complex account of how male bodies are discursively shaped by psycho-social and historical processes. (Connell, 2000) Masculine bodies are given social meaning through a variety of disciplinary practices that regulate the body, like sporting exercises, repeated patterns of violence, work practices or military drills. However, these processes of masculine embodiment are passive and mechanical. Bodies aren't blank pages on which pre-determined meanings and stories are written. Bodies, in reality, are much more active agents in these processes: wriggling, refusing, colluding, acquiescing. As a result, embodied masculinities are always the dynamic sites of many colliding social forces, contradictions and surprises.

Furthermore, we need to look more closely at the heterosexualising and masculinising of men's bodies and subjectivities. The normalising and naturalising of heterosexual masculinities is dependent on an oppressive Othering and demonising of gayness. Rigid polarities and binary divisions are constructed between straight and gay masculinities, and these are rigidly policed. A supposedly complete biological dimorphism reinforces the perceived superior power of heterosexual masculinity, assuming it to be fixed, unchanging and natural. (Collinson and Hearn, 1996)

Normative heterosexual masculinities are constantly threatened by femininity, gayness and other forms of more fluid, plural sexualities that look as if they might dissolve the tightly locked and policed boundaries between straight and gay sex. That's why there is a constitutive denial and often brutal disavowal of potentially disruptive Otherness (femity and gayness) that is central to the formation of heterosexual masculinities. (Collier, 1998, p60) Consequently, any hints of weakness, vulnerability or femininity are often ruthlessly expelled from uncontaminated straight masculine identities and projected onto subordinated Others, frequently through violent homophobic action.

It's important to recognise that young men's understandings of what it is to be properly masculine varies according to social class background. (Laberge and Albert, 1999) While middle-class boys and men are more likely to value leadership, sociability and intelligence as a part of their commitment to future economic and social mobility, working-class boys value displays of physical strength, bravery, looking 'cool' and proving their attractiveness to girls. Many of the traditional masculinity-accomplishing processes for young white working-class men, in a context of de-industrialisation and unemployment, have vanished. Perhaps new forms of working-class masculine self-identity have emerged in their place, closely linked to youth styles, fashion and consumption. (Collison, 1996) Although positioned in economically and socially subordinate ways, some white working-class young men seem to use style and fashion as a form of exaggerated masculine display to counter their lack of social power. Indeed, presenting yourself as 'flash' and 'making it' is important to many young working-class men in shaping new versions of themselves that give them back some street respect and peer group status as reflected in the eyes of the male gang. (Collison, 1996)

The Suspects

The central part of this article is based on the police surveillance video transcript (PSVT) and the Martin Bashir interview with the suspects on *Tonight*.

The PSVT was the result of the police bugging of Gary Dobson's flat in December 1994. Brian Cathcart has described, in some detail, what happened through the bugging period: "For a few weeks, starting on 2 December, the police listened to, watched and recorded the suspects and their friends as they came and went, watched television, listened to music, cooked, chatted and larked about." (Cathcart, 1999, p223) The tapes comprised dozens of scenes from inside the Footscray Road flat featuring Neil Acourt, Gary Dobson, David Norris and Luke Knight, as well as their friends Charlie Martin and Danny Caetano and one or two others. (Cathcart, 1999, pp231-232)

The young men recorded on the audio and visual probe seem to be aware that they are being bugged, and to some extent played up to it, but this didn't seem to inhibit them in their aggressive, sometimes wild, physical and linguistic behaviour. There were no admissions of guilt on the tapes, but they contained uncensored evidence of the everyday actions, relations, attitudes and behaviour of the suspects.

The PSVT has given us a rare and startling look into the lives of the suspects. It has also given us some detailed evidence of the "subculture of obsessive violence, fuelled by racist prejudice and hatred" (MacPherson, 1999, p5) that permeated the everyday lives of the suspects.

Before the full engagement with the PSVT, here are some of my initial, personal impressions of the lives of the suspects and a detailed exploration of the social backgrounds of the suspects and the specific localities within which they lived.

I am haunted by the image of Neil Acourt, one of the suspects, leaving the 1998 public inquiry. (Cathcart, 1999, pp210-211) This was the judicial public inquiry into the Stephen Lawrence case, chaired by Sir William Macpherson. Its terms of reference were: "To inquire into the matters arising from the death of Stephen Lawrence on 22 April, 1993 to date, in order particularly to identify the lessons to be learned for the investigation and prosecution of racially motivated crimes." The five suspects attended the inquiry on June 29th and 30th, 1998.

Acourt's body language shows a swaggering confidence, as if he believes he is beyond the reach of law and order. He reminds me of smirking, bully-boy faces from my own secondary school, faces that I could never relax around. I felt like I was holding my breath when I was in their company, waiting for the next barbed action or the mocking, ridiculing voice that would expose my vulnerabilities in front of all the rest of the boys.

Acourt doesn't shrink back from the jeering crowd like an apologetic criminal. Wearing dark glasses and with his hands held out and his palms upwards, he looks like the smiling hero of a film première, rather than a prime suspect in a murder inquiry. He blows kisses to the hostile onlookers, appearing to revel in the attention. He looks as if he's saying, "Come on then! I can take on all-comers! Just try me!" But that heroic front is deceptive. The media have over-emphasised the arrogance of the suspects. Neil Acourt isn't just a 'bloody-minded thug', as D.C. Davidson suggested in the Macpherson Inquiry. (Macpherson, 1999, p146) Instead, he is a man who seems to be full of contradictions and uncertainties, and his attempts to deny his anxieties and defend himself from his imagined fears of masculine and white inadequacy involved him in a frighteningly brutal, racist murder. This study will relate the heroic swagger to the suspects' anxieties in order to understand and challenge why they might have killed Stephen Lawrence.

In *Routes of Racism*, Roger Hewitt comments: "[Anti-racist] strategies should incorporate an understanding of how these young people [racists] live and how they see the world, and not be based on how those 'in authority' would like them to think and live." (Hewitt, 1996, p59)

I think Hewitt is right. No amount of moralistic preaching at young white racist boys and men will change how they view the world. Instead, what needs to be done is to get beyond our initial recoil of disgust and anger, and base our future anti-racist strategies on how white racist boys in south-east London make sense of their inner and outer worlds, why they invest emotionally in violent, self-aggrandising identities, and trace exactly how and why they actively participate in a world of extreme racist violence. It's not possible to change something without first noticing what's actually there and then burrowing below the surface to find out why it's there.

There are enormous gaps in our understanding of the aggressively racist motivations of young white working-class boys and men, particularly those living in the outer city. This critical investigation, although tentative, is an attempt to fill in some of those gaps, so that future anti-racist work with white boys and young men can concentrate more effectively on what needs to be changed.

The Specific Localities and Social Backgrounds of the Suspects

Eltham, where Stephen Lawrence was murdered, is a surprising, contradictory place. When I visited Eltham in September 1991, I expected to see urban grimness and poverty. But on Well Hall Road and the Progress Estate I was met by mock-Tudor fronts, hanging baskets, mullioned windows and ornate carriage lamps. Owner-occupiers were tending neat, trimmed lawns. It was a fantasy of pastoral village England in a place that you pass through on the way to somewhere else. It looked like a place that wanted to associate itself with rural Kent than see itself as a part of inner-city London. But these predominantly white outer-city neighbourhoods, where four out of the five suspects lived, now make up some of the most "dangerous and difficult localities for racial minority communities." (Hewitt, 1996)

Eltham is in the borough of Greenwich in south-east London, where racial harassment and extreme racist violence are commonplace. In one year, "440 [racist] incidents were reported to the police, one of the highest levels in the country, and by common consent this was a fraction of the total." (Cathcart, 1999)

Racist violence in Greenwich is not a new problem. Hewitt recalls compiling a dossier of incidents collected in 1980 that could have been written today:

"Mr. X was washing his car on Sunday [...] and a group of young boys came along, using racially abusive language, picked up the bucket and threw dirty water on him."

"Mr. Y was chased by a group of white youths and was hit. He escaped by taking shelter in a house. Later his car was rammed on a second occasion."

"Mr. Singh was resting on a bench with his eyes closed. A bunch of white youths came and took his turban and ran away." (Hewitt, 1996)

Greenwich Action Committee against Racist Attacks (GACARA) kept regular statistics of racial victims over a period of six years from 1990–1996. Despite different statistical methods, "all the figures show an unacceptably high, and continuing, level of attacks. GACARA recorded 1013 for 1996." (Jeffrey, 1999)

In specific sites in Eltham, there was the 'marking out of 'white territory' by adolescents wishing to claim the area as exclusively theirs. Some sites were particularly conspicuous for their racism, such as the churchyard of Eltham parish church. This is what Hewitt and his researchers found there just a few months after the murder of Stephen Lawrence: "The churchyard of Eltham Parish Church suffered from much racist grafitti and damage, including gravestones inscribed with 'Kill All Blacks', 'BNP', 'NF', 'KKK' and even a drawing of a masked skinhead in Nazi salute beside the inscription: 'British Arian race and nation'. Large swastikas were daubed on some very old graves and for several weeks the white gate at the side-entrance to the churchyard, which faces out onto Eltham Hill, displayed a foot high swastika beneath which were written the words: 'Watch out coons, your now Entering Eltham.'" (Hewitt, 1996, pp20-22) The Progress and Brook estates, although places that declare themselves as exclusively white territories, do not make up a classic area of social deprivation.

The schools that the suspects attended (Kidbrooke and Crown Woods) are not sink schools, but have a relatively progressive reputation. Indeed, the schools were some of the first mixed-sex comprehensive schools to be "purpose-built in this country, for the postwar influx of tenants from slum clearances." (Jeffrey, 1999)

The history of the Progress and Brook estates is revealing. The start of the First World War in 1914 gave rise to the rapid expansion of the workforce at the Woolwich Arsenal complex, producing howitzers for the Western Front. They urgently needed houses, and Eltham was the chosen location. In 1915, the Progress Estate started with 1,298 family houses built in a Garden City style. The adjacent Brook Estate was a later addition, built in the 1940s and 1950s as a part of a slum clearance programme. (Cathcart, 1999, p20-21)

Local housing practices, since the Second World War, have created "patterns of residential segregation" (Jacobs, 1999) that have partly made it possible for the Brook Estate to become a white racist enclave. While black households have been largely restricted to the inner and middle bands of British cities (often because of the racist assumptions of local housing officers), outer-city estates like the Brook have become mainly associated with white working-class families. The result has been the construction of a territorial polarisation in some areas, putting up a mental and physical barrier between white and black communities.

As Keith Jacobs comments: "Both Woolwich Borough Council and its successor Greenwich Council, formed in 1965, operated housing-allocation policies that privileged existing tenants. Their 'sons and daughters' scheme (whereby tenants' children on the waiting list were given priority when properties became vacant) meant that estates such as the Brook continued to house indigenous communities and exclude others." As a result, the Brook Estate was generally perceived as a 'no-go' area for black people, and was a place where white paranoia about an invasive black menace could thrive.

So the suspects had a contradictory class position. They weren't your typical working-class urban poor. And the suspects certainly didn't view themselves as bottom of the heap. Sandwiched between the relative prosperity of Kentish suburbs like Bromley and Orpington and more socially depressed areas like Woolwich or Thamesmead, the suspects seemed to be very much aware of their own transitional, borderline class positions. Perhaps they wanted to be seen as confident, 'flash' and 'making it'. But they also saw daily evidence of the defeated and the failed. So perhaps they were also possessed by fears of falling back, of becoming 'losers'? As a result, the suspects dressed smartly, had slicked-back hair and deliberately dissociated themselves from working-class, skinhead culture. Indeed Neil Acourt, on the PSVT, refers to "... all those fucking yobbo fucking skinheads...".

Some of the suspects had another point of social difference. Because of the Acourts' and Norris's connections with the southeast London criminal network their families were atypical of local estate associations. (Jeffrey, 1999) And David Norris lived in Bromley, a possible result of his father's criminal, but financially successful, drug-dealing and gun-running.

Some parts of Eltham became white enclaves, pockets of extreme racism, in a much more culturally diverse mosaic of neighbourhoods within the borough of Greenwich. Many white working-class boys saw Eltham as exclusively white turf to be defended against 'foreign' invasion from without. This defensive paranoia is a key element in understanding the intense and widespread racism of the youth culture in Eltham and Greenwich. Its ferocity surprised Roger Hewitt and his researchers: "In some neighbourhoods it seemed that open and unapologetic racism was wall to wall amongst adolescents, with almost no gaps. Indeed, it was apparent that what we were dealing with was a local culture of racism that was deeply entrenched." (Hewitt, 1996)

This specific 'culture of racism' worked through racist jokes, graffiti, rhymes and songs that made up an "oral culture of racist communication which circulated in the peer groups and families of the area." (Hewitt, 1996) However, this adolescent racism wasn't just passed on through the family, but seemed to be generated and maintained through internal and external policing within local peer groups.

The Young, White, Male Loser Discourse

Many white, working class boys in south-east London, like the suspects, seem to be afraid of being seen as 'losers'. Many of the traditional sources of masculinity-accomplishing processes for young, white, working class boys like apprenticeship schemes, manual labour in manufacturing industries, and violent, dangerous action within the armed forces (fighting inter-state wars rather than negotiating complex peace-keeping missions like in Kosovo) have been closed down.

Alongside these masculinity losses, rapidly changing cultural and social developments have undermined the certainties of a mythic, English way of life. These social shifts and erosions work on three main levels: the multicultural, the European, and the destruction of the national myth of the unified nation, now threatened by devolution. (see Hall (1999)) The visible presence of racial and ethnic diversity on the streets of south London, the challenges to a traditional English nationalism presented by the movement towards being a part of Europe, and the break-up of the taken-for-granted myth of the single, white, unified nation by the processes of devolution in Scotland, Wales and perhaps Northern Ireland — all these social and cultural changes indirectly and directly affect young white working-class men in their loosening sense of identity.

From the detailed evidence of the PSVT, many of these boys and young men appear threatened by a loss of meaning in their masculine identities, their masculinised and heterosexualised bodies and their whiteness. In terms of jobs, income, reputation, bodily performance and style, their lives are characterised by fears of disintegration and anxiety. These recent social upheavals have called into question their traditional rights to be proud of being white and English, their assumed right to feel harder and superior to everybody else, and their right to go on calling themselves 'masculine'. The imaginary fear of having a 'naturally privileged' place in the world abruptly usurped by potential competitors is very much with them.

Some of the main contemporary sources of their insecurities are described below.

Unemployment and De-industrialisation.

There has been an historic collapse of heavy industry in the local area. The Greenwich area was famous once for work in the docks, shipbuilding, labour on the railways and in military-related industries of armaments, engineering and metal-working. Woolwich Arsenal once employed a workforce of 80,000. (Hewitt, 1996 & Jeffrey, 1999) Job losses, especially for male working-class labourers, have been sweeping.

Male unemployment in the Eltham area remained high, "keeping steady at over 20% for a generation." (Jeffrey, 1999) This meant a severe narrowing of scope for white working-class boys in the area. Young boys and men can no longer identify themselves as hard or 'masculine' through the physical strength and endurance involved in the manufacturing industries. Perhaps some of these boys feel an increasing sense of pointlessness and lack of purpose. They fear the sense of aimless drifting, and they don't have any secure anticipation of a future that they can play an active part in.

Work for some of the suspects, in the 1990s, was on an occasional and patchy basis. "Leaving school was a matter of finding a job through a network of relatives and friends, and this for many boys was preceded by perhaps a year or more of occasional and unofficial work side by side with a brother, uncle or father." (Hewitt, 1996, p11) Neil Acourt got a job as a drayman at a bottling and soft drinks firm run by two uncles in Woolwich when he left school. (Cathcart, 1999, p27)

Academic Failure

The suspects were all low achievers at school. Getting through school as quickly as they could and getting out into the world seemed to be more important to them than learning. Nick Jeffrey comments that there is a "real south and east London belt of young male failure, black and mainly white (sic)." He goes on to say that the "GCSE exam results published for that string of schools in Greenwich and Lewisham are among the lowest in the country for attaining five grades A-C; a very low 10%." (Jeffrey, 1999)

The suspects all left school, or were excluded or expelled, without any educational qualifications. They seemed more interested in getting a dangerous reputation and displaying that they were the 'hardest cocks around' than being troubled about academic failure. But also it's important to acknowledge that achieving status through frequent disruption, gang violence and knife and weapon use could also be seen as a defence against being seen as 'losers.' Their local reputations as unpredictable 'nutters' mattered a great deal to them. As one of the informant's notes verifies (about Morris and Neil Acourt): "... they are very dangerous knife users who always carry knives and quite like using them.' (see Cathcart (1999), p53)

There was a common pattern in the five suspects' school careers of extreme violence, exclusion, bullying and expulsion. Norris was permanently excluded from school for "persistent, uncontrollable, disruptive behaviour." (Cathcart, 1999, p28) Jamie Acourt became involved in fights with black boys at school. One local black boy called Sean Kalitsi was accused by Jamie of 'giving the lip' to a friend, and in the resulting fight Jamie knocked Sean down a flight of steps. Jamie was excluded from school for five days and then, after a monkey wrench was found in his school bag, he was permanently excluded. (Cathcart, 1999, p27)

The Perceived Undermining of White Privilege

Luke Knight said, in the interview with Martin Bashir, "... the reason why I said things against black people was because I believed black people ruined my life at the time." (*Tonight*, April 8 1999, Granada)

Some white working-class boys in south-east London are not only confronted by the fear (real and imagined) of being seen as failed or lost boys, in terms of education, father absence and work, but also have to come to terms with their unconscious fears of being 'ruined' or usurped by a fantasised, black menace. There are local and national strands that make up these anxieties and fears.

The Local Context

Les Back's research on white racism in south-east London found that many white working class boys were both fascinated and threatened by young black masculinities. (Back, 1994) Perhaps some white boys envied young black men's greater symbolic and cultural resources? As Stuart Hall suggests. "In music, fashion and street culture, minority youth have acquired a 'leading-edge position', symbolically if not materially." (Hall, 1999) Some aspects of black masculine culture not only possessed a seductive appeal in terms of its adventurous innovation of popularly-acclaimed youth styles and music, (Back, 1993) but it was also seen as "undesirable, dangerous and aggressive." (Back, 1994) As a result, some white working-class boys felt an uncomfortable mixture of fear and desire for fantasised black men. This ambivalent, suppressed desire for blackness is at the heart of the envy and fascination some white working-class men and boys feel in relation to young black masculinities. The 'black wannabe' longing is often just under the surface of their noisy hostility towards black people.

Some young white men try and strenuously establish the security and coherence of hard, white, embodied English identities through denying the existence of the racialised Other in their lives. (see Frosh, Phoenix and Pattman, 1999) But envious, unconscious longings to be black (often fantasies of physical strength, coolness and sexual prowess etc.) are often there waiting to take their revenge, even in the 'hardest' of brave, white, English fronts.

The mounting shame and self-disgust associated with these unresolved longings to be black present difficult problems for insecure white men. Their fears of being failed, white, working-class men, experienced in their hidden inner worlds, gives rise to a violently intense repudiation of blackness in the public world. This produces a powerfully charged emotional energy that is often used to defensively justify the uncontaminated nature of their supposedly pure white, hard Englishness.

So perhaps at the centre of the suspects' actions are their urgent attempts to deny their own confusing, ambivalent desires about fantasised black men? As Robert Young suggests: '...we find an ambivalent driving desire at the heart of racialism: a compulsive libidinal attraction disavowed by an equal insistence on repulsion.' (Young, 1995)

On the PSVT, the white suspects appear obsessed by and envious of black masculine style. Underneath the persistent repetition of abusive phrases like 'black cunts' you can also hear a much more ambivalent approach being worked out. The suspects seem locked into a competitive battle with young black men (again, at a real and imaginary level) about the right to go on living their apparently solid and coherent white masculine identities. It's as if they can't fully acknowledge the contradictory realities of young black men's lives without destroying who they think they are. Take the suspects' responses to the Malibu advert they watch on TV, for example:

> Gary Dobson: "Look I think this is racist this advert."
> Luke Knight: "Yeah all white people sad and all that."
> Gary Dobson: "And yeah look all power station in the background and the niggers all got beaches, sunshine, fucking."
> Luke Knight: "You couldn't do it the other way round."

The more the suspects envy a fantasised, black way of life ("... the niggers all got beaches, sunshine, fucking."), the more they are aware, relationally, of intensified white loss. To openly confront the white loss in their own lives would endanger the stability of their own identities, so they displace that threat onto black men, and imagine black people are stealing away white vitality and energy. As Luke Knight suggests ("You couldn't do it the other way round."), there is a binary system of fantasised extremes that constructs imagined white loss or unfairly treated white victims ("... all white people sad and all that.") in relation to imagined, black triumphant potency.

Within that closed binary system, the suspects are desperate to re-assert white masculine hardness and heterosexual potency. In the end, the only way the suspects perceive they can do this is through violent, racist attack. And this involves projecting their own fears of being 'losers' onto the black men that they attacked.

The intensity of the suspects' responses to the fantasised black threat comes through forcefully in the PSVT. The sexual potency threat is clear enough in the Malibu advert response above, and it is associated with the suspects' anxieties about and fascination with black men's physical size, their masculine hardness, their cool style and their aggressiveness.

The irony is that actual black men's lives are much weaker than the inflated fantasies of some white men would have us believe. The difficult contradictoriness of some black men's lives is being masked by these white men's fantasies. Many white men (like the suspects), although openly contemptuous about black men, also seem to unconsciously idealise them. They would also like to be 'top dogs' — apparently 'rock-hard', cool, sexual winners. They fail to recognise the changing complexity and diversity of black men's lives — the cool, brave front sometimes hiding real pain, the everyday ache of white institutional racism, the struggle to survive and keep their self-respect, are all disguised under the carapace of seeming hardness.

Here, the suspects seem awed and diminished by the physical presence and the size of some black men they encountered:

> Neil Acourt: "Was he a big cunt."
> Charley Martin: "Yeah a big nigger."
> Neil Acourt: "What a big cunt."
> Charley Martin: "Yeah a big nigger."

The almost dazed repetition of 'big' here underlines the imagined threat of young black men supposedly invading the 'naturalised' tightness of the suspects' white superiority and the security of their physically embodied, masculine identities. It's the solidity and hardness of their embodied identities where the threat strikes most deeply. The suspects' grip on the physical solidity of who they think they are seems in danger of being eroded. And there is also the anxiety, eating away at their confidence, that these black men might actually be harder than them if it came to a fight. Perhaps that's why the suspects try and defend themselves through the abusive put-down shown by the repetition of 'cunt' and 'nigger'. They cover up their anxieties through effeminising ('cunt') the imagined black menace and also reducing black men to an inferior slave position ('nigger').

The hardness of their heterosexualised masculinities is also severely challenged by their fearful imaginings connected to the black, male bouncer look:

> Charley Martin: "Like when you see him straight away you don't like the look of him."
> Neil Acourt: "He's a bouncer."
> Charley Martin: "No this one he was a big cunt he'd all gold on him and everything."

The fantasised black menace is primarily seen, by the suspects, as a bodily threat to their white integrity. For example, Neil Acourt's outburst in praise of Enoch Powell indicates what's really at stake here:

> Neil Acourt: "I wanna write him a letter Enoch Powell mate you are the greatest, you are the don of dons get back into Parliament mate and show these cocksuckers what it's all about, all these flash, arrogant, big-mouthed, shouting their mouths off, flash, dirty, rapists, grass cunts…"

Acourt seems physically assaulted by the fantasised threat of black style, black sexual potency and heterosexuality, black culture and black bodies. His own intactness and coherence as a white working-class man seems in danger of being dismantled, so he defends himself through homophobic abuse ('cocksuckers') and savagely aggressive racism. His hysterical tirade of race hatred reveals the extent of his own insecurity and his frustration about not being heard. In this case, his insecurity is revealed through having to promote Enoch Powell as a potential advocate rather than believing that he could speak out himself.

The suspects' worries about street style are also apparent. The repetition of 'flash' above in Neil Acourt's speech and the reference to 'gold' on page 13 of the PSVT, indicates the suspects' competitive rivalry with black, masculine style. The more flamboyant, black style is experienced as a direct affront to the suspects' status. Whereas some of the suspects strive for a smart, affluent style that is conspicuously designer-label aware, with Versace jumpers and a 'nice pair of boots', some black men seem more spontaneously confident in their invented idioms. They seem to have more street credibility than the suspects, who are more concerned with giving an appearance that they've made it.

Their white insecurity is also displayed in the suspects' inability to accept black winners. In fact, they compete with black men about who defines the terms of reference within which white/black are defined as losers/winners. The suspects expend a great deal of emotional energy in wanting to keep black men down as black losers. The suspects are so frightened of being elbowed out of their 'naturally' privileged positions that their prevailing tone is stridently defensive. This can be seen most clearly in the suspects' responses to the TV treatment of the Cameroon football team, winning the lottery and the *Sports Personality of the Year* competition.

About the Cameroon team:

> Luke Knight: "... why the fuck should he [a television commentator] want niggers to win it when they're playing something fucking like Italy or something like a European fucking team..."

About the lottery:

> Charley Martin: "It's got to be a white."

About the *Sports Personality of the Year*:

> Neil Acourt: "A macroon better not win it mate."

Black athletic prowess, like in Linford Christie's case, is also seen as directly eroding white, masculine identity. The suspects are worried about Linford Christie's chances of winning the *Sports Personality of the Year* award.

> Luke Knight: "I guarantee I know who wins it — Linford fucking Christie."

The implication here is that it's a white establishment conspiracy that is favouring Christie's chances, rather than real ability. Perhaps the suspects even feel betrayed by the fantasised white nation?

The ponderously elaborate joke told against Linford Christie by Danny Caetano, on page 15 of the PSVT, is a bid to undermine Christie's champion status as a black runner. The joke focuses on Linford Christie being chauffeur-driven in a limousine. It's late and

Christie arrives at a hotel to get a room for the night. The hotel manager refuses Christie access to the main hotel, telling him that the hotel rules say that if you're black you've got to go round the back. Christie says, "Do you know who I am?" The manager replies that he recognises Christie as a champion runner so it won't take him long to get round the back, then, will it?

The joke tries to turn the tables on Christie's reputation as a winner and very fast runner, and attempts to fit his running ability within a reductive, black loser framework. And there are also some suggestions of homophobic put-down here as well. The suspects' attempt to reclaim white men's superiority merges with a heterosexual supremacy. Supposed black losers, like Christie, have to repeatedly 'go round the back', sexually as well.

> Danny Caetano: "Sorry mate like that's the rules your black you've got to go round the back."

The presence of black winners, like Linford Christie, threatens the very existence of the white suspects. The suspects seem to face a bleak either/or choice in their imaginations. Either they are recognised as white winners or they are nothing. Black men must be seen as losers for white men to be 'somebody'.

The National Context

The historical decline of English imperial power and cultural authority has left a legacy of uncertainty in young white men like the prime suspects. In a way, they don't know how to be white English men any more. In humiliating economic and social circumstances where they often feel like failed men, some white working-class young men, living in outer-city pockets of extreme racism, feel those past visions of white English supremacy and greatness slipping away from them, however unconscious those processes might be.

Blackness and Englishness are still mutually exclusive categories in the white man's imaginings. (Gilroy, 1987) As more and more black people take an active part in reworking the British way of life, so the suspects' fantasies about the true English nation possessing an essential core of uncontaminated whiteness became defensively embattled. Perhaps they believed in that mythic notion of white English purity being invaded by what they might have construed as an anti-English, black menace. The worst nightmare scenario for the suspects was picturing a horde of black 'foreigners' stealing away their rightful place in the world, stealing their jobs, their homes, their girlfriends, their possessions, and their exclusively white territory.

In praising Enoch Powell on the PSVT, some of the suspects describe their fears like this:

> Luke Knight: "... [Powell] was saying no I don't want them here no fucking niggers they'll ruin the gaff and he was right they fucking have ruined it."

There has also been a white backlash against multiculturalism. For some white working-class boys it has seemed that other cultures have been excessively celebrated and given preferential treatment at the same time as white English culture has been ignored. In terms of white national identities this has involved having to confront loss and decline, and perceiving that their own culture is more like a negative absence than a positive assertion of anything.

As Roger Hewitt suggests, "For some white English pupils, the celebration of cultural variety actually seems to include all cultures that are not their own. It is not surprising that white children — especially, it seems, young people from working-class homes, experience themselves as having an invisible culture, even of being cultureless. White pupils, to some extent, seem like cultural ghosts, haunting as mere absences the richly decorated corridors of multicultural society." (Hewitt, 1996)

Certainly, on the PSVT, the prime suspects express open hostility to what they perceive as the rhetoric of multiculturalism:

> Neil Acourt: "... listen we don't want to take all this nigger bollocks no more, we can't even say black ball, black cat, this, that."

They reject multiculturalism's celebration of a cultural diversity that has left them feeling like 'cultural ghosts'. They react violently against school pressure to conform to politically correct language that respects cultural diversity. Neil Acourt speaks out of a passionate resentment about what he perceives to be "unfairness to whites." (see Hewitt, 1996)

The White Warrior Discourse

In the previous section, I showed how the suspects' anxieties were connected to a psychic and social destabilising of white working-class embodied masculine identities. Their anxieties were particularly provoked by their everyday encounters with cultural, racial and ethnic differences that they didn't seem able to cope with.

The suspects' desires for a more solid masculine embodiment and a more certain subjective position in the world seems under constant attack from fantasised black men's presences. What seems to directly undermine them are their fears and anxieties, extravagantly enlarged in their imaginations, about black men's physical size, their sexual potency, their masculine hardness, their cool style and their supposed hyper-aggressiveness.

In order to understand the suspects' defensive paranoia here, I want to approach their anxieties and counter-assertions through a psycho-social exploration. In this exploration I will draw upon a Kleinian psychoanalytic perspective (Mitchell, 1986; Frosh, 1987; Dawson, 1994) to interrogate the defensive construction of white warrior masculinities that are identified through attempting to protect themselves from the threat of disintegration. I will connect those processes of defensive construction to the lives of the five suspects.

Confronted by the fears of disintegration resulting from the male loser discourse, the suspects, perhaps unconsciously, wanted to reconstitute themselves as vigorous, manly and powerfully dominant, especially in their gendered selves and white English identities. That involved a psychic struggle to secure and consolidate white masculine identities, but it also involved a social struggle for approval and recognition. Anxieties that are potentially self-annihilating are also results of social anxiety (about unemployment, academic failure etc.) as much as internal doubts. (see Frosh, 1987)

The suspects defended themselves from the disintegrating effects of anxiety through psychic splitting. (A friend (Tony Jefferson in a personal communication) has suggested that, in strictly Kleinian terms, the suspects might have "remained in the paranoid-schizoid position where black people were concerned i.e. they projected their 'bad parts' onto the black Other and attacked it there." In other words, they have failed to achieve the ambivalence associated with the depressive position (at least in this area of their lives.)) They expelled all the threatening bits of their lives and projected them on to imagined masculinities that were constructed as weaker and subordinate. It seems likely that these imagined masculinities were mainly black. The suspects strived to define themselves as flawlessly white, hard and English through projecting their ambivalence and self-doubts onto put-down, racialised others. They attempted to build a white warrior coherence through denying their loss and projecting it onto fantasised black men.

To protect the integrity of the threatened self, a person's inner and outer worlds can be split into 'good' and 'bad' figures. In this specific case, it seems possible that the prime suspects divided their inner and outer worlds into idealised and persecutory figures. Like in the Malibu advert example, above, fantasised black masculinities were viewed as imaginary enemies, or persecutors, defined against a frustrated, unachieved vision of idealised, white purity and coherence. But in their actual lives they couldn't put into practice that reassuring vision, except through acting out in the outside world their triumphalist, white, warrior fantasies. (see Daniels, 1997)

In building a new sense of white masculine identity, the suspects' fears and insecurities had to be displaced onto the invaded, disempowered body of a black man. Indeed, in order to construct their own power, the white suspects needed to select a black man as prey who appeared less visibly armoured and perhaps more vulnerable than many other black men. Perhaps Stephen Lawrence became their chosen prey because he appeared more innocently vulnerable than other, more trouble-aware, black men?

Stephen's friend, Duwayne Brooks, who escaped with his life, thought that it was Stephen's lack of hardness and street knowledge that might have made him a target for the suspects. Duwayne says: "There was a group of us, and [Stephen] was the softest person out of all of us — not physically, he was stronger, fitter than me — but his mind was softer." (The *Guardian Weekend* magazine, April 1 2000)

In plunging their knives into the body of Stephen Lawrence, the white suspects might have been reconstructing themselves as white, heroic warriors in relation to a defeated, powerless, black masculinity. They were no longer failures to themselves, in their imaginations, because they had triumphed over their imagined persecutor. They had made an exhibition of their bodily hardness and aggressiveness, and provided visible proof that black men were wrong when they thought "that they were harder than us."

The full horror of what they actually did in killing Stephen Lawrence seems to me to be hidden from the five white suspects. By being preoccupied with re-establishing their own coherence and unity as physically embodied white warriors, they dehumanised Stephen Lawrence as the racialised Other. They appeared to be more concerned with managing their own psychic conflict. So they didn't see the real Stephen Lawrence on the morning of April 22nd,

1993, anxious about his father and full of hope about being an architect. They didn't see his concern about getting back late after his mother had asked him to be back home by 10.30. All they saw was a negative stereotype, a black persecutor who had stalked them in their paranoic imaginations. They saw a psychic obstacle that had to be defeated if they were ever going to feel sure and certain in their embodied white masculinities. That fixation prevented the suspects from acknowledging the full brutality of their action.

In terms of the suspects' need for social approval and recognition, the killing of Stephen Lawrence can also be seen as a desperate bid for a 'hard case' reputation and status in the local community. The Acourt brothers and Norris all strove to be seen as a part of a hard-man culture of dangerous violence, like the legendary Kray twins, or Clifford Norris, David's criminalised father.

In a way, the suspects wanted to be seen as dangerously violent defenders of white territory. Indeed, on the *Tonight* interview with Martin Bashir, Neil Acourt described himself as a "natural defender, a defender of myself." As we have seen already, the local youth culture in Eltham and Greenwich displayed an extreme and widespread racism. To gain recognition in that social context, perhaps meant denying uncomfortable feelings of defeat and loss through acts of wildly uncontrolled racist violence. Neil Acourt and David Norris painting a three-feet-high NF slogan on the wall of the local youth club was an early movement in that direction. (Cathcart, 1999, p29)

Academic failure at school was reconstructed by gaining a heroic reputation through unpredictable, excessively violent behaviour. We've already heard about Jamie Acourt's fights with black boys and his aggressive confrontation with Sean Kalitsi. But it was the obsessive and often frenetic use of knives and other weapons that really established their names in the local community.

The suspects, especially the Acourts and Norris, seemed to be continuously competing for the 'hardest lad' reputation. They achieved this reputation through being prepared to use knives to kill and maim, to go further than anybody else to defend white masculine honour from imagined insult. They became familiar in their estate communities as "well-known 'nutters' with knives." (Cathcart, 1999) They were also referred to as "very dangerous beings" in one of the informants' notes left on the windscreen of a police car on April 24th, 1993. (see section 13.29 of the Macpherson Inquiry report) They got this local reputation through a long string of stabbings and knife attacks on people like Stacy Benefield, Lee Pearson, the Witham brothers, Gurdeep Bhangal, as well as Stephen Lawrence. (Cathcart, 1999, pp80-86) As 'knife-obsessed racists' they gained local hero-worship through being able to intimidate their enemies, carry out racist violence, and avoid legal punishment. As Sam, an Eltham resident commented: "l think the people they hang out with sort of hero worship them. I just don't go into the pubs where they go. Everybody round here wants to be a gangster... l think their friends hero worship them." (Wilson & Chaudhary, *The Guardian*, February 25 1999)

Peer group dynamics and power relations within their gang also helped the Acourts and Morris to fashion and sustain a white warrior status, indeed, without the regular peer group bolstering, the attack on Stephen Lawrence might never have happened. In the PSVT, a great deal of time is spent on sorting out a pecking order hierarchy within the group. Neil Acourt continually tells off Gary Dobson for allowing the landlord in while no one was there, perhaps to bug the flat. Gary Dobson spends a lot of time trying to fit into the group, but comes over as apologetic and wary, especially in front of Neil Acourt.

Luke Knight, although much more angrily vociferous in his racism, is also an odd one out in the group. Neil Acourt polices the internal hierarchy of the peer group by patronising and humiliating Luke. At one point in the PSVT, Neil Acourt says to Luke: "Start talking little man" (page 14) and again: "Luke you're going red mate." Of course these remarks are deliberately meant to insult Luke's masculine identity. The implication is clear; 'real' men have some proper size and blushing is only for girls.

Both Neil Acourt and Norris inflate their gang-leader status by telling competitive stories about violence, fighting and knife attacks. They both seem to be disciplining the peer group hierarchy through the threat of imminent violence. Neil does that through a physically restless, prowling movement around the flat attacking walls and armchairs, and rehearsing knife attacks on group members, and then authoritatively instructing learners in the group how to use knives: "Just go dig straight in deep." (page 15)

Their stories are bragging monologues to establish group position, demonstrating their shockingly brutal bravado and their fantasies of aggressive domination. They hush the rest of the group into deferential silence. Both Norris and Neil Acourt forge superiority and a leadership position in the peer group through their manic outbursts of self-dramatising, masculine, bodily performance:

> Neil Acourt: "I reckon that every nigger should be chopped up mate and they should be left with (nothing but) fucking stumps." (page 9)

and:

> David Norris: "I would I'd go down Catford and places like that I'm telling you now with two sub-machine guns and I'm telling ya, I'd take one of them skin the black cunt alive mate, torture him, set him alight." (page 51)

But beneath these in-your-face, bragging monologues, it's possible to detect a more hesitant note. This comes from a defensive necessity to talk themselves up, to create self-protective fantasies of aggressive manly omnipotence. The feverish tone of their stories also hints at the way those unachieved visions of idealised white purity and coherence will always remain unattainable. This is particularly true in David Norris's monologue, with its repetitive attempts ("I would...

I'm telling you... and I'm telling ya...") to convince himself and the peer group of his own bodily solidity and status as a self. You can hear again that pleading note. The anxious insecurity indicates, again, that the boasting tries to construct a defence against the perceived threat of masculine and white inadequacy.

Conclusion

"If we are to challenge racism successfully in the domain of popular discourse, we must place an understanding of gendered processes at the centre." (Les Back, from *The 'White Negro' revisited*, 1994)

The most neglected areas of investigation into Stephen Lawrence's murder are whiteness and embodied masculinities. Not just whiteness by itself, or masculinities alone, but the dynamic, complex interactions between whiteness, race and the bodily struggle to become masculine in a specific locality in south-east London. As Les Back says above, if we are to understand and change what the suspects might have done, we have to bring gendered processes more into the picture, alongside race and class. The suspects' searches for a more stable and certain grip on their whiteness, hardness and Englishness, at a time of rapid cultural and social change, is at the heart of the reasons for Stephen Lawrence's murder.

This psychic and cultural destabilising of some white working-class masculine identities is closely related to the enormous changes and diversity lived through in Britain over the last twenty years. A severe crisis of English and white identity, in a post-colonial context, has interacted with the losses and shocks undergone by traditional heterosexual masculinities over the same period.

Stuart Hall puts it like this:

> Social, economic, cultural, technological and moral shifts, unsettling established patterns and norms, have combined with Britain's relative economic decline, the unrequited loss of imperial destiny and the onset of globalization, which

relativizes the power of the nation-state and national culture, to produce nothing short of a crisis of British, and especially English, identities. What does it mean to be 'British' in a world in which Britain no longer rules the waves? (Hall, 1999)

In pockets of extreme racism, like the Brook estate in Eltham, these shifts and cultural differences (multicultural drift, Europe, and devolution) have deepened the threat to insecure white and masculine identities. In some young white men's imaginations, their 'rightful' and superior place in the world is now in danger of being usurped by black 'foreigners', cultural differences and loss of traditional working-class employment.

The killing of Stephen Lawrence is closely linked to this perceived erosion of white working-class heterosexual male dominance in some areas of outer-city racism. This threat to their taken-for-granted sense of white masculine superiority is intensified by the anxiety that black masculine bodies pose to the security and boundaried solidity of white English embodied masculinities. The white working-class hierarchy of bodily hardness, sportiness, sexual prowess and coolness has been radically called into question by white men's inflated perceptions of black masculinities as super-masculine and super-sexual. As a result, old assumptions of white working-class masculinities being harder and braver than any other masculinities are in the process of fracturing and breaking apart. In emasculating circumstances, where white working-class men are confronted by loss, failure and dishonour, in bodily and social terms, the suspects defended themselves from disintegration through attempting to turn themselves into white warrior embodied masculinities. (Daniels, 1997) This reframing process, from perceived humiliated failures to imaginary, chivalric avengers (Messerschmidt, 1998) reaffirming white honour and bodily supremacy, is at the heart of the reasons for Stephen Lawrence's murdered. And in bodily terms, the suspects were trying to give new substance and coherence to their threatened, anxious bodies. Through the extreme violence of their bodily actions they were trying to re-establish white masculine honour through the reconstruction of their failed bodies. And that could only be achieved through reframing the power relations between white and black men's bodies.

The act of knifing is a resource for overcoming perceived threat. The knife penetration of Stephen Lawrence is really about beating back the imaginary challenge of black bodies through associating his penetrated body with effeminacy and loss of power. (Daniels) The fantasised black man has his mythologised strength and genital potency stolen away from him, in a similar way to the close connection of castration and lynching in the southern states of the U.S. (Messerschmidt, 1998) White supremacy is constructed and re-affirmed at the point where the black man's body is penetrated, feminised and subordinated. The killing of Stephen Lawrence represents a bid to re-establish and reproduce race and gender hierarchies at a turbulent time when these traditional hierarchies and divisions are perceived to be being undermined. (Messerschmidt, 1998) The prime suspects were perhaps trying to recreate unequal racial and gendered boundaries again between white and black men by allocating a subordinated status to black men through violence and intimidation. And, of course, there are bodily implications to these re-positionings as well. Stephen Lawrence's murder also represents a bid to re-solidify (through the qualities of hardness and potency) shaky, white bodies at the expense of a penetrated, disempowered black body. This extreme, racist violence, now being experienced all over Europe, urgently needs to be understood as a desperate bid to fortify insecure, white, embodied masculinities.

This anxiety and perceived threat has led to many white working class men making deep emotional investments in a 'monolithic whiteness' (Brah et al, 1999, p11) and rock-solid, supposedly invulnerable masculine identities. Any challenge to the stability of their identities, such as living through the ever-changing swirl of multicultural relations in south London, is hysterically denied through brutal and vicious repudiation. So any anti-racist approach that works with young, white, racist men needs to try and transform these emotional investments in 'monolithic', hard, white, English identities. An over-rational perspective that questions racist attitudes and beliefs doesn't really stand a chance because it doesn't recognise the complex, emotional formation of these white, racist identities. At some point, it's necessary to work with these underlying fears and anxieties about being seen as humiliated white losers that motivates many young white working-class men today. It's this fear of loss (in terms of work, fathers and parents, hardness, whiteness and Englishness) that needs to be worked on, emotionally, before they can stop believing in the fantasy promise of racist identities that will give them back a proud completeness and coherence in an apparently dissolving world.

As Peter Redman remarks: "If boys and men are to disinvest from existing forms of heterosexual masculinity (and existing forms of white racism), then they will need alternative ways of making imaginative sense of the social and psychic contradictions that their existing identities address." (Redman, 1996, p177)

What we need now are alternative sources of masculine identification, so that young English men (especially in the 14–25 age range) can break out of the narrowness and rigidity of present white English masculine identities. We need a much wider range of masculine identities that aren't so threatened by difference; identities that more open to Otherness and difference, and that don't compulsively need to constitute themselves in opposition to feared, imaginary enemies. Can we imagine different kinds of masculine identity that can learn to live with a great deal of social flux and fragmentation and real and imagined loss? Can we visualise masculine identities that can accept that anxiety, grief and loss are an everyday part of being masculine?

Positive, alternative masculinities today need to be able to tolerate much more fluid boundaries between hardness/softness, black/white, heterosexual/gay etc., and the self and the Other.

Certainly we don't want a fixing of a subordinated and estranged Other as a way of securing and firming up shaky and insecure selves. Indeed, some of these narrow, racist identities seem unable to live with contradiction, variety and ambivalence. Instead, they defensively construct themselves in hierarchical relation to a feared and despised Otherness. We urgently need a non-binary treatment of the Other, that doesn't try to fix or dehumanise the Other as 'irredeemably different.' (see Silverman and Yuval-Davis, 1999, p43)

Confronting whiteness can be seen as a practical way of refusing to dehumanise the Other. Whiteness is still largely invisible in our culture and we urgently need to explicitly problematise it as a racial/ethnic category rather than expending an over-concentration of effort on blackness. Anti-racist work in educational institutions needs a "more sensitive and sophisticated approach to questions of white ethnicity." (Gillborn, 1995) Some detailed historical enquiry would help in uncoupling English whiteness, with its traditional and reactionary associations with nationalism, imperialism and racism. But monolithic versions of white identities also need to be critically deconstructed and changed. A very useful perspective on deconstructing whiteness has been suggested by Anoop Nayak. He reports on an educational project that investigated the "diverse histories of white students upon Tyneside" through sharing their own personal biographies. This led to some of the students looking a bit more closely at the hybrid and diverse history of English identities. From this unusual perspective, Nayak claims that "imploding white ethnicities offered a way of contextualising anti-racism." (Nayak, 1999)

In the end, the challenge to young white racist men is clear. However much they try and expel their fears of Otherness and difference onto an imaginary black menace, those hidden fears and anxieties will always return to haunt them. The reason for that inevitability is that the source of this constructed, racialised Other is already within them, in their fears and anxieties about their own lives. No amount of violent, frustrated struggle can produce a pure, totally intact, white English hard self that is totally separated from a demonised, racialised Other. Perhaps real courage, these days, in the lives of young white racist men like the suspects, is shown not through being knife-obsessed racists but through turning and facing these fears of Otherness and difference within themselves?

References

Back L. (1993) 'Race, Identity and Nation within an Adolescent Community in South London', *New Community* 19 (2): 217-233.

Back L. (1994) 'The "White Negro" Revisited: Race and Masculinities in South London', in Cornwall A. and Lindisfarne N. (eds) *Dislocating Masculinity: Comparative Ethnographies*, London: Routledge.

Blair M., Gillborn D., Kemp S. and Macdonald J. (1999), 'Institutional Racism, Education and the Stephen Lawrence Inquiry', *Education and Social Justice* 1: 3, Stoke on Trent: Trentham books.

Brod H. (1987) 'The Case for Men's Studies', in Brod H. (ed.) *The Making of Masculinities: The New Men's Studies*, Allen and Unwin.

Cathcart B. (1999) *The Case of Stephen Lawrence*, London: Viking Books.

Collier R. (1998) *Masculinities, Crime and Criminology*. London: Sage Publications.

Collinson D. and Hearn J. (1996) 'Men at 'Work': Multiple Masculinities/Multiple Workplaces', in Mac an Ghaill (ed.) *Understanding Masculinities*, Buckingham: Open University Press.

Collison M. (1996) 'In Search of the High Life: Drugs, Crime, Masculinities and Consumption', *British Journal of Criminology*, Volume 36: 3.

Connell R.W. (2000) 'Globalisation and Men's Bodies', in *The Men and the Boys*, California, USA: The University of California Press.

Daniels J. (1997) *White Lies: Race, Class, Gender and Sexuality in White Supremacist Discourse*, New York: Routledge.

Dawson G. (1994) *Soldier Heroes: British Adventure, Empire and the Imagining of Masculinities*, London: Routledge.

Dyer R. (1997) *White*, London: Routledge.

Frosh S. (1987) *The Politics of Psychoanalysis: an Introduction to Freudian and Post-Freudian Theory*, Macmillan.

Frosh S., Phoenix A., Pattman R. (1999) '"But It's Racism I Really Hate": Young Masculinities, Racism and Psychoanalysis', *Journal of Psychoanalytic Studies*.

Frosh S., Phoenix A., Pattman R. (2002) *Young Masculinities*, Palgrave.

Gillborn, D. (1995) *Racism and Antiracism in Real Schools*, Buckingham: Open University Press.

Gilroy P. (1987) *There Ain't No Black in the Union Jack*, London: Unwin Hyman and Routledge.

Hall S. (1999) 'From Scarman to Stephen Lawrence', *History Workshop Journal*, Issue 48, Autumn 1999, Oxford University Press.

Hewitt R. (1996) *Routes of Racism: The Social Basis of Racist Action*, Stoke on Trent: Trentham Books.

Jacobs K. (1999) 'Institutional Housing Practices and Racism: the Brook Estate, Eltham in *History Workshop Journal*, Issue 48, Autumn 1999, Oxford University Press.

Jeffrey N. (1999) 'The Sharp Edge of Stephen's City', *Soundings*, Issue 12, Summer 1999.

Laberge S. and Albert M. (1999) 'Conceptions of Masculinity and Gender Transgression in Sport among Adolescent Boys', *Men and Masculinities*, 1.

Macpherson Inquiry, *JSO*.

Messerschmidt J. (1998) 'Men Victimising Men: The Case of Lynching, 1865-1900', in Bowker L. (ed.) *Masculinities and Violence*. California, USA: Sage Publications.

Mitchell J. (ed.) (1986) *The Selected Melanie Klein*, Penguin Books.

Morgan D. (1993) 'You Too Can Have a Body Like Mine: Reflections on the Male Body and Masculinities', in Scott S. and Morgan

D. (eds) *Body Matters*, London: Palmer Press.

Nayak A. (1997) 'Frozen Bodies: Disclosing Whiteness in Haagen-Daz Advertising', *Body and Society*, 3:3.

Nayak A. (1999) 'Pale Warriors: Skinhead Culture and the Embodiment of White Masculinities', in Brah A., Hickman M., Mac an Ghaill (eds), *Thinking Identities, Ethnicity, Racism and Culture*, Basingstoke: Macmillan Press.

Nayak A. (1999) 'White English Ethnicities': Racism, Anti-racism and Student Perspectives', *Race Ethnicity and Education*, 2:2.

Petersen A. (1998) *Unmasking the Masculine*. London: Sage Publications.

Redman P. (1996) 'Empowering Men to Disempower Themselves: Heterosexual Masculinities, HIV and the Contradictions of Anti-oppressive Education', in Mac an Ghaill (ed.), *Understanding Masculinities*. Buckingham: Open University Press.

Rutherford J. (1997) *Forever England: Reflections on Masculinity and Empire*, London: Lawrence and Wishart.

Segal L. (1990) *Slow Motion: Changing Masculinities, Changing Men*. London: Virago Press.

Silverman M. and Yuval-Davis N. (1999) 'Jews, Arabs and the Theorisation of Racism in Britain and France', in Brah A., Hickman M., Mac an Ghaill (eds.), *Thinking Identities: Ethnicity, Racism and Culture*, Basingstoke: Macmillan Press.

Theweleit K. (1987) *Male Fantasies. Volume One. Women, Floods, Bodies, History*, Cambridge: Polity Press.

Transcript of a compilation video of intrusive surveillance conducted on the five suspects, as seen by the Inquiry (1999) from *The Stephen Lawrence Inquiry: Appendices*, TSO. Referred to in the text as the PSVT.

Young R. (1995) *Colonial Desire: Hybridity in Theory, Culture and Race*, London: Routledge.